Engineless narrowboat butties were still being built in the 1950s to a design first used 150 years before. These boats were launched sideways. This one is the 'Raymond', built for Samuel Barlow & Co Ltd in 1958 at Braunston. The prow, stern, rudder and cabin were decorated in a style at least a hundred years old.

CANAL ARTS AND CRAFTS
In memory of Howard Lansdell

Avril Lansdell

Shire Publications Ltd

CONTENTS

Published in 1997 by Shire Publications Ltd, Cromwell House, Church Street, Princes Risborough, Buckinghamshire HP27 9AA, UK. Copyright © 1994 by Avril Lansdell. First edition 1994, reprinted 1997. Shire Album 300. ISBN 0 7478 0233 5.

Printed in Great Britain by CIT Printing Services, Press Buildings, Merlins Bridge, Haverfordwest, Pembrokeshire SA61 1XF.

British Library Cataloguing in Publication Data: Lansdell, Avril. Canal Arts and Crafts. – (Shire Albums; No. 300). I. Title. II. Series. 745. ISBN 0-7478-0233-5.

ACKNOWLEDGEMENTS

No book can be written entirely alone and the author wishes to record her thanks to Hilary Broadribb, for her help in typing and organising the text, and to Sidney Renow for printing her photographs. Thanks are also due to Karen and Phil Lea, for permission to quote their research, and for the cover and other photographs. Thanks are given particularly to the staff at the three main waterways museums: to Tony Hirst, Lynn Doylerush and Peter Bursnell of the Boat Museum, Ellesmere Port, to Laurence Cook, Ann Rayson and Margaret Ratcliffe of the Canal Museum, Stoke Bruerne, and to Tony Condor and Roy Jamieson of the National Waterways Museum, Gloucester, for help in research, assistance in taking photographs, and for finding other suitable pictures. Others who helped me can be seen in the list of names below.

This book was researched and written with the encouragement of British Waterways staff, especially Vanessa Wiggins, their Media Relations Executive.

Photographs and other illustrations are credited as follows: Harry Arnold Waterways Images, pages 4 (bottom), 12 (middle right); The Boat Museum, Ellesmere Port, pages 16 (bottom left and bottom right), 21; British Waterways Archives, pages 7, 10 (bottom), 14 (bottom), 20 (top), 23 (bottom left), 25, 28 (top), 30; Leslie Bryce, ARPS, page 30; *Coventry Evening Telegraph* and the Boat Museum, pages 1, 12 (top); Joan Gregory, page 6 (bottom); Herefordshire Record Office, page 9 (top); Mrs Kathleen Irving, pages 6 (top), 23 (bottom right); A. F. Kersting, FRPS, and the National Trust, page 4 (top); Mr and Mrs P. Lea, cover and pages 20 (bottom), 23 (top); *London Illustrated News* and British Waterways, page 5; Hugh McKnight Photography, page 18; Hugh McKnight's collection, pages 19, 27; Derek Pratt Photography, page 8 (top); Mrs Janet Reeve, page 24 (top); Cadbury Lamb, pages 8 (bottom), 17 (both), 24 (bottom), 31 (both); Mr and Mrs M. Turpin, page 26 (bottom); *Waterways World*, page 6 (top). All other pictures are by the author, including the drawing on page 3.

A cottager and his family outside their door in 1790. They lived by a river or a canal and people like these became the first boaters. Their children and grandchildren left the cottage to live on the narrowboats in the 1820s and 1830s. This sketch is based on an oil painting by George Morland which is now in the Royal Holloway College Picture Gallery.

INTRODUCTION

The distinctive lifestyle of the people who lived and worked on the narrowboats of the English canals evolved, blossomed and disappeared over a period of just under two hundred years. In its time it changed as much as the lifestyle of any other group of English working people. What made the boat people different from any other group was that, by being itinerant, they became a fairly self-contained group of families, known to each other and to other workers with whom they came into regular contact while at the same time remaining mysterious to outsiders, especially the middle classes, who avoided them or romanticised them because their environment and personal possessions, such as boats, domestic utensils and, even-

tually, clothes, were distinctive and different.

Boats on the early canals were manned by men and boys whose families lived in cottages, usually on the edges of towns. Most eighteenth-century boatmen made day trips, apart from the crews of the 'fly' boats whose double crews of young men made longer trips, working day and night to reach their destination and return in as short a time as possible. These men returned home at weekly or fortnightly intervals. The boatmen were land-based and enjoyed a higher standard of living than that of farm or factory workers. Like many other cottagers of the late eighteenth century, they had painted panels as pictures in their rooms, lustreware china or brass

3

The great houses of the
eighteenth century had rooms
decorated with mouldings and
panellings painted with formal
designs of flowers and
picturesque ruined palaces, as
in the dining room of Saltram
House, Devon, designed by
Robert Adam in 1768. The
roses and castles of the
narrowboats probably
originated in this aristocratic
taste and filtered down
through the social classes
over a period of fifty years,
being carried out in different
materials to result in a
colourful exuberance that
echoes the same satisfying
balance of design.

This twentieth-century narrowboat cabin is on the
'Friendship', now in the Boat Museum at Ellesmere
Port. It has stylised floral decorations on wood-grained
panels on the walls and a painting of a castle on
the hinged panel between the cabin's two beds, which
are set at right angles to each other. This small flap
was incorporated in narrowboat cabins after the Canal
Boats Act of 1877, which required that these beds be
separated from each other by a solid partition. It
is swung back out of the way in the daytime, when the
side bed becomes a seat.

This print, published in 'The Graphic' in 1875, shows the interior of a narrowboat cabin looking out through the doors to the tiller. There is no detail of decoration, although the side bed/seat and the table/ cupboard can be seen, as can the bottle stove. Cooking would have been done in a saucepan or cooking pail set on the ledge in front of the stove's open door. The interior of the crockery cupboard can be seen on the right. The boatwoman's larder was in the small triangular space below the tiller and its closed doors can be seen through the cabin doors across the small deck.

jugs as ornaments, patchwork quilts on their beds and cage-birds as pets. Their clothes were the same as those of other country and working-class people. Boats were owned either by canal carrying companies, such as Pickfords, or by individuals, known as 'number ones'.

In the early nineteenth century this prosperity was followed by a drastic decline. Railway competition forced the carrying companies to cut wages and a boat captain could no longer afford to employ a crew and pay rent on a cottage. Many families moved on to the boats in the years between 1820 and 1840; the wife and a child formed the crew, becoming the 'mate' and 'boy' respectively. Although the boats had been brightly painted before this time, they had been in plain, solid colours. The decorations, which reflected popular working-class art of the time, were added to the boats in this period.

It was not a move for the better. In the middle of the nineteenth century the boat people grew poorer and poorer. The paintings faded; their living conditions were overcrowded and insanitary; disease and drunkenness were rife, mortality high. Only when laws were passed to improve the boat people's conditions, to increase their pay and to give their children a better education did the pride of the boaters return. Their heyday was the late 1880s and the 1890s and the companies and the boaters of this time repainted their boats and other possessions. The clothes that are now known as the 'traditional' clothes of 'the cut' (the boaters' own name for the canals) are the clothes that were worn in the 1890s and early 1900s. This was a second period of prosperity for the boaters and they continued to wear these same clothes in the fresh period of decline that followed it simply because they could not, then, afford new ones. Their children, from about 1913, tried to be 'fashionable'– as working people reckoned fashion – but, in many cases, they ended up looking poorer than their parents.

These same decorations of boats and domestic utensils, derived from the 1890s, have now come to represent the heyday of the canals and to be regarded as the 'traditional' arts of the boaters. It is generally reckoned that the boats owned by 'number ones' carried more decoration than those owned by the commercial companies, although both were used as the boaters' family homes.

Today, with the increasing use of the canals for leisure and holidays, boat own-

Mrs Kath Irving of Burton, South Wirral, at a boat rally at Hockley Port in 1980. Mrs Irving, a schoolteacher, made her own costume; it was so much admired that she afterwards made replica 1890s boaters' clothes for many other modern men and women. At this, her first rally, it was a very windy day and she tied the strings of her bonnet beneath her chin to keep it on. An elderly boatwoman told her that most 1890s boatwomen, who wore their hair in a bun at the back of the head, tied the strings of their bonnet at the back, below the bun. This pulls the bonnet front well down over the forehead to shield the eyes in the sun or rain.

ers and hirers are reviving the 1890s decorations on boats and boating accessories, albeit, in many cases, with commercially produced transfers rather than hand painting. At popular boat rallies, organised by the Inland Waterways Association, prizes are awarded to the best-decorated boats and the best-dressed crews, who often wear boaters' costumes of the 1890s.

The traditionally decorated domestic items are also popular in modern homes, while the designs, motifs and colours are used in modern embroideries. The canal museums are among the most popular of English tourist attractions.

Howard and Avril Lansdell in 1984. Both are wearing replica canal costume of the 1890s, which includes a shirt embroidered with scarlet feather stitching and a flower-sprigged bonnet.

6

Typical 'Monkey boats' at Islington Lock on the Regent's Canal in 1823. The boats are plain, with no decoration other than the company's name and the boat's name and number. These loaded boats are 'sheeted up', their cargo hidden below canvas sheets tied up to, and draped over, the top plank. The lock keeper is gauging the depth the boat is floating in the water in order to calculate the weight of the cargo and the subsequent toll to be paid.

THE NARROWBOATS

THE BOATS

Although a great many different boats, mainly floating boxes with no decking or cabins, were used on the newly constructed canals, by the end of the eighteenth century the standard canal boat was 72 feet (21.9 metres) long and 7 feet (2.1 metres) wide, with a small foredeck at the prow and a cabin at the stern. This had a small deck between the cabin doors and the rudder post, leaving room for the tiller which steered the boat. This style of boat had been designed and built by Thomas Monk of Tipton and was at first known as a 'Monkey' boat. Later the same type of boat, with slight variations, was built at boatyards up and down the canal system and the name adopted for all of them was 'narrowboat'.

The floating boxes were towed in long strings by varying numbers of horses or bow-hauled by teams of men, but narrowboats were usually worked in pairs known as 'butties' (from an old English word meaning 'mates'). One horse or two mules could pull both boats, the box-mast used as the towing point being in the centre of the front boat, a third part along.

By the end of the nineteenth century many pairs were composed of an old-fashioned butty pulled by a diesel motorboat, which differed from the butty by having slightly less cargo room, since extra cabin space was needed for the engine. When specially built, rather than converted from a horse-drawn boat, they were made of steel and had a different shape of tiller.

The butties were built from planks laid edge to edge and the decorative painting was confined to the areas above the waterline. The hull was black, but the upper parts of the prow were brightly col-

7

A pair of well-painted narrowboats photographed at Hawkesbury Junction in 1982, showing the traditional decoration on prow and cratchboard. Behind the cratch the decorated box-mast and two decorated stands to support the top plank can be seen in the empty holds. When the boats are empty, access to the holds can be had through a door in the engine-room or cabin.

This picture shows the construction of the forepart of the hold of an unladen boat. The cratch was not just an upright board, but a three-dimensional structure designed to support and shape the canvas sheeting over the cargo. The decorated back edges of the cratch and the decoration on the box-mast and stands show only when the boat is empty or unsheeted. This picture also shows how the planks are fitted on to the mast so that they do not slip. At the stands they are overlapped.

oured. Curving lines running back from the prow towards the stern formed an enclosed band along the gunwale on which were painted swags of roses and/or geometric symbols. The small foredeck, which sometimes covered a tiny cabin, ended in an upright cratch, or triangular structure, designed to support the top plank of a gangway running along the length of the boat above the hold. The cratch was decorated with diamond shapes painted in bright colours and panels of roses. As the cratch and the prow were the first part of an oncoming boat to be seen they were as eyecatching as possible. Red, white,

blue, yellow and green were the predominant colours.

The canvas sheeting drawn up to the gangway over the cargo was either black or green; behind this, the stern cabin was as brightly coloured as the prow and cratch.

The cabin sides were divided into panels, the largest of which was lettered with the owner's name, registration town and other details. A smaller panel would be decorated with a landscape scene, and another small panel with the boat's registration number. The frames of the coloured panels were wood-grained. The cabin roof

This photograph shows the difference in shape between the rudders and tillers of the motorboat (right) and the butty (left), the butty being far more massive than the iron motorboat. The roof of the motorboat cabin is longer than that of the butty because it covers the engine-room as well as the cabin. The ventilator over the engine was known as the 'pigeon box' and was often decorated quite lavishly. This pair are company boats with the livery of Fellows Morton & Clayton. Decoration of these boats was confined to the interior of the cabins.
This photograph comes from the Stingemore Collection in the Hereford Record Office. It was taken on 19th June 1937 by F. H. Stingemore, the artist who designed the map of the London Underground that has been in use for many decades, and who took many photographs of canals.

The National Waterways Museum has on display the cabin, stern and rudder of the 'Cylgate', a wooden butty of c.1900. This photograph shows its rudder adorned with a horse's tail. The tiller has been removed in this display so that visitors can see into the cabin (see top photograph on page 15).

Only at night, or when the boat is left unattended, are the cabin doors closed. This reveals the back of the cabin, which is always painted in two colours, usually with a third colour introduced as a narrow dividing line, in a flowing arabesque arch shape. The Midlands boaters call this shape 'the mouse's ears'. The design has many variations, but the outer colour is the same as the surround on the cabin sides, and the decorative line disguises the plain shape of the cabin.

9

The rudder post and tiller of a modern horse-drawn trip boat on the Monmouth & Brecon Canal. While the rudder post is as brightly painted, the tiller is not as long or as elegant as on the older Barlow and Fellows Morton & Clayton boats (see photographs below and opposite top).

was painted with plain red oxide, as was the interior of the hold, or with a plain green or blue gloss paint. The stern bulkhead, including the doors giving access to the rear cabin, was painted in two colours divided by a flowing arabesque. The sliding hatch above the cabin doors was painted with a simple geometric block design or a symbol from a playing card. The boat's name appeared on a curving band of colour on the stern gunwale, similar to the band with decoration on the prow. Forward of the name the band continued in a decorative pattern to the junction with the hold. The tiller of a motorboat was made of tubular steel, painted like a barber's pole, but the tiller and rudder of the butty were a massive wooden construction. The rudder was painted plain black, but the rudder post was brightly decorated with geometric symbols and embellished with ropework.

The tiller was removable, set into the post so that it curved down to the steerer when in use. At night the tiller could be

removed altogether or reversed in its socket so that it curved upwards, out of the way of people using the cabin doors.

CANAL-BOAT LETTERING
The lettering used on boats always had at least two colours in each letter. It was important that it could be seen and read easily from a distance. It changed slightly over the years of the nineteenth century to become the typical late Victorian decorative lettering also used on tradesmen's

Barlow boats were always noted for their decoration, this small family company being as proud of their boats' appearance as any 'number one' owner/boater. The lettering on this 1950s boat is blocked on the right. While blocking is always done below the letters, to 'lift' them up, it can be used on either side, according to the style favoured by the owner of the boat or the signwriter. The tiller of this boat is in the 'travelling' position, arching downwards.

Fellows, Morton & Clayton Ltd's boats were painted black and white until the mid 1920s, when these colours were replaced with red and green. The wooden butty 'Northwich', now moored in Gloucester Docks as part of the displays of the National Waterways Museum, has been restored to her 1920 colours and fittings. The white lettering is blocked on the left in pale blue against a black ground. The surround is white with a red line marking out each section. The name of the boat is painted in white on black at the stern, with no blocking. On the prow the name is painted in blocked letters on the raised sides of the fore cabin. The sliding hatch above the cabin doors and the cabin block supporting the top planks each have a red centre on a white shape against a black background. The tiller is in the 'at rest' position, reversed in its socket so that access to the cabin is easier.

carts and shop fronts. The nineteenth-century signwriter had a steady and respected job; his work has lingered longest on the canal boats and has been continued and improved by his successors. In the 1890s there were several favoured styles of lettering, the simplest being a sans-serif block alphabet with a contrasting line round each letter. More common was the use of wider lines on one side and below each letter, giving a three-dimensional effect. Victorian signwriters were familiar with several variations of this lettering. Different boatyards had different styles of lettering, those in the south being the simplest. Some of the northern yards used a derivative of a style called Tuscan, turning its leaf-shaped serifs into round knobs which gave a very decorative appearance.

The large carrying companies each had their own house style of lettering proclaiming their identity.

ROSES AND CASTLES

The decorative style of painting used on canal boats was not naturalistic. Its origins lie in the painted panels used as pictures in eighteenth-century cottages and on cottage furniture, some of which were similar to peasant art in several European countries. The flowers used were mostly roses, although daisies and sunflowers were also common. Each petal was formed by a single and separate brush stroke, the darker colours put on first and the highlights last. Leaves were added afterwards and the leaf veins were the final touches, worked from the centre outwards. Flowers were always formally arranged in

This magnificently painted boat shows all the traditional decorations. The rudder post has a compass star on its side; the curving tiller is painted in at least two different colours. The open cabin doors show castle pictures at the top, and flowers in a recessed panel below them. The little canvas cloth, placed over the gunwale to keep the capping clean, is also painted with flowers. The gunwale itself carries a row of diamonds and another compass star. A large castle picture is painted on the side of the cabin beside the panel proclaiming the owner's name. The stove chimney carries three polished brass rings, and two painted watercans and a mop are in their traditional places beside the chimney. Many boatwomen picked wild flowers to stand in a jar on the cabin top.

In 1948, after nationalisation, the British Waterways Board's boats were all painted yellow with blue lettering. This was extremely unpopular with the boaters, even though the boat doors were redecorated by Tom Ditton, the painter at Balls Bridge yard. By 1950 the colours were reversed to blue, picked out in yellow, and standard transfers were used inside the doors. These transfers can be seen in this view of the 'Tarporley' in 1963. Although the transfers had been designed by Frank Jones, a painter from Leighton Buzzard, their universal use meant that the variety and spontaneity of boat painting was in danger of being lost. In the late 1960s the Board relaxed this rule and those boaters who remained on the cut lost no time in repainting their decorative panels by hand. Transfers, however, are still available and are used on many hire boats today.

Many boatmen were themselves skilled painters. A highly decorated boat would have flowers in all conceivable places. This is the top surface of a tiller, at the end where the thick arm becomes the prong to fit in the socket of the rudder arm. The whole tiller has been painted with daisies in two colours. It was probably the work of a number one. Some boatwomen, too, were as good at painting flowers as their menfolk.

The view from the deck, down into the cabin of the 'Northwich', reveals the side bed on the right and the edge of the stove on the left. Beyond the stove is the closed table/cupboard and beyond that again the cupboard holding the rolled-up bedding. Below this cupboard, which is hinged at the bottom to provide a support for the mattress, is a large drawer, with a corresponding large drawer under the end of the side bed. The top of the side bed, nearest the stern of the boat, has a lift-up lid to the locker below it. At the far end of the cabin is the door to the hold.

bands or in massed clumps. The stems of the flowers were not shown.

The landscapes in the panels outside and inside the boats were always fantastic dream-like scenes featuring a river or a stream, usually with a bridge of some sort, and with a building – a fairytale castle or, less frequently, a Tudor farmhouse – as the main subject.

These panels were painted in strict order: first the sky, then the hills, then the river and the foreground, with the bridge and the castle last. Colour was solid and brush strokes were firm. Highlights and small details were put on last. Everything was simplified, the overall effect being the most important.

CABIN INTERIORS AND DECORATIONS

The interior of the boat cabin, 10 feet (3.0 metres) long, 7 feet (2.1 metres) wide, $5^1/2$ feet (1.7 metres) high, was painted in brown paint 'combed' with graining tools to resemble wood graining. The layout of the boat cabin became standardised over the years and every boat family kept the same things in the same place. A double bed at the end of the cabin next to the engine-room in a motorboat or the cargo hold in a butty boat was let down out of a cupboard at night, so locking the engine-

room or hold door. The side bed, at right angles to the double bed, became a seat during the day. The door of the cupboard between the double bed and the kitchen range let down to form a table, with a drawer and a smaller cupboard below against the cabin wall.

All cupboard doors and drawer fronts were made with recessed panels and narrow mouldings. Large areas of the inward-sloping walls were also panelled, as

All Fellows Morton & Clayton boat and butty cabins were painted inside with light brown paint with a 'combed' woodgrain finish. There was usually a castle painting on the table/cupboard door and on the insides of the double doors to the cabin and decoration on the coalbox (see page 14, top). Any other decoration had to be added – or paid for – by the family who lived in the boat. Many of them added roses round the castle on the table/cupboard and a further castle picture on the door to the hold, while number ones' cabins were often even more elaborately decorated.

13

Even into the 1920s the cabins of company boats were equipped with a bottle stove, like this one in the 'Northwich'. If a boat family wanted a kitchen range, which would include a small oven, they had to buy and fit it themselves. This bottle stove of 1920 is no different from those installed in narrowboats fifty years before. The cabin's coalbox was a drawer under the deck and its end, covered by a plank, made a step down into the cabin. The ends of these coalboxes were always decorated and could be very picturesque, carrying a playing-card symbol or, as on this one, the simple design that was part of FMC's company livery and was repeated on the cabin block (see page 11, top). The 1920s boatwoman's larder was housed in a small triangular cupboard at the base of the rudder post, similar to that of the 1875 boatwoman (see page 5).

were the rear door of the cabin into the hold or the engine-room and the two smaller doors forming the entrance from the stern of the boat, each of which was divided horizontally into three sections. The middle section was panelled and recessed. The top and bottom sections were flat.

Decorative fairytale castles in imaginative landscapes were painted on the top section of the door panels. The centre panels and the wall panels within the cabin were painted with motifs of roses and other flowers, as were drawer fronts and cupboard doors. The outside of the table/cupboard door was also painted with a landscape and castle, which showed when this door was closed. The interior of the cupboard and the table top were painted as a wood grain.

The floor of the cabin was covered with linoleum, often in a pattern resembling tiles or large checks.

A fully furnished cabin was always highly decorated. The possessions which other working people spread out around a small cottage were packed together in a space 10 feet by 7 feet (3.0 by 2.1 metres). The boatwomen were very houseproud and most boats and cabins were spotlessly clean in spite of the long working hours and the dirt of many common cargoes, such as coal. Brass oil lamps, stove guards and airing rails, polished every day, complemented the shining black-leaded stove or range. Horse brasses, trivets and brass doorknobs were favoured ornaments as they would catch and reflect light. 'Lace' plates with pictorial centres have become associated with narrowboats as much as the painted roses and castles. This photograph shows the interior of the 'Sunny Valley' on show at the Canal Museum, Stoke Bruerne.

14

BOAT UTENSILS

The boaters' domestic utensils of all kinds were painted with flowers and geometric patterns. The coal bin, which was a large drawer under the double cabin doors, formed the step down into the cabin. It usually had a playing-card symbol on the end of the drawer, but some boaters preferred flowers or a castle. Small stools were decorated all over. Kettle boards and bread boards were decorated on the back, and even storage chests were painted all over. The dipper for taking water from the canal had a painting on the base as well as the sides.

The big, decorated fresh-water cans and the mop used to wash down the boat were normally kept on the cabin top rather than inside. Also on top of the cabin was the cabin block, which supported the stern end of the top plank over which hung the tarpaulin sheets which protected the cargo. The decorated metal nose can used to hold the feed for the boathorse was also laid on top of the cabin at night.

The handbowl or dipper, used for taking water out of the canal for many purposes, was usually plain inside. On the outside it was painted with roses and other flowers on the sides, and with more flowers or a picture on the base. The dipper was hung in the cabin, between the stove and the door, so its base was a natural focal point for a picture. Some dippers had castles on the base, but many had portraits of dogs, horses or men. The sailor from the Players' cigarette advertisement was very popular, as were cavaliers or knights in armour. This dipper is very restrained in its decoration, which consists only of roses set in scalloped panels defined by yellow and white paint.

This cabin block is on display in the Canal Museum at Stoke Bruerne. It supported the end of the top plank on the cabin roof (see page 11, top). This one shows yet another variation in the style of castles used on boats, boatyards or painters having their own individual style.

This painted foghorn, now at the Boat Museum, was used in misty or foggy weather. The plunger on the top of its pump (left of picture) blew a note through the horn to let boaters know that another boat was travelling on the canal. The pump is decorated with a spray of roses, but the horn carries spiralling stripes. These multicoloured stripes were also used on mop handles and the iron tillers and rudder posts of the motorboats (see page 9, top and bottom).

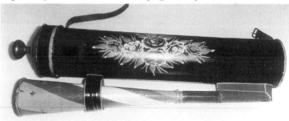

Oil lamps were used as bulkhead lights on wooden horse-drawn boats travelling through tunnels or in the dark. This one came from the 'Aries' and is painted with roses and daisies. It is now in the Boat Museum at Ellesmere Port.

16

ROPEWORK

Rope has an important function on any boat and on canal boats it was used in many ways: the boats were towed with rope lines; rope was used to tie up the boat and to secure the cloths over the cargo. It was possibly the early boaters' pride in keeping the lines securing the cloths neat and tidy that brought about the decorative ropework now associated with the narrowboats.

In the early days, a vast array of differ-

Right: *Motorboats did not carry as much decorative ropework as the butties, although the metal tillers may carry a Turk's head to stop the steerer's hand from slipping. Motorboats had large fenders at the back, made from skilfully knotted rope, stuffed with odds and ends of worn rope. These were held to the stern by chains, and this picture shows two types of knotted fender on motorboats seen at the Wendover Arm Festival in May 1993.*

This modern canal houseboat has a front cockpit with a protective tarpaulin over a top plank behind a decorated cratchboard. The tarpaulin is fastened up to keep it out of the way on a sunny day. The prow of the boat carries a wide flat fender of knotted rope. This boat was photographed at the Rickmansworth Canal Festival in May 1993. The mooring rope has been looped several times between the mooring stake on the bank and the fore-end stub on the boat, then secured with two half-hitches. The same type of fender and mooring would have been used on a working narrowboat.

17

The 'Titania' is an example of a boat with good decorative ropework. The plaited crown around the top of the rudder post is known as a 'Turk's head'. There is a smaller one around the tiller, next to the rudder post. On the rudder post there are decorative coils of rope each side, held in place by a rope binding. A long knotted tail of rope connects the ram's head (the top of the rudder post) with the rudder blade. This ornamental rope is known as a swan's neck. It is a practical use of macramé knotting, with loops each end. It is wider in the middle, where it is held out by an inserted plug of smooth wood. This centre is decorated with a smaller Turk's head. At the top of the rudder blade is a round fender known as a monkey's fist. Boaters made their own fenders and rope decorations, teaching their children the same skills. The smaller hands of children were often better at the more intricate knotting of a little Turk's head than those of their parents. Both men and women made the decorative ropework, although men usually made the large fenders.

ent types and thicknesses of rope was used on canal boats. Over the years rope made of cotton came to be standard. A cotton rope will stretch and therefore takes up the strain slowly, whereas sisal rope may break if a sudden strain is put on it. Cotton rope will wear and break and can be spliced to hold firm again. Worn rope ends could be used as the stuffing for fenders, while broken tow-ropes can be reused as Turk's-head plaits or swan-neck decorations. These were usually made by the boatmen for their own boats.

All ropework decorations on a narrowboat were kept clean by scrubbing. The sun bleached them white, and they showed up well against the brilliant paintwork or darker tarpaulins.

This young couple, photographed in 1902 on the Regent's Canal, wear the clothes that have now become the traditional clothes of 'the cut' (the boaters' own name for the canals). They are very similar to the basic clothes of working-class people of the 1890s and the boaters continued to wear them into the twentieth century. This distinguished the boaters from the people on the bank and the out-of-date clothes became associated with the narrowboats. While most country girls wore sun-bonnets, they wore them well back on their heads. An 1890s country youth would not have worn the large neckerchief of a boatman with its ends pulled out through the waistcoat armholes, neither would he have had a waistcoat with a velvet collar, for the young boater is wearing the uniform first issued to Fellows Morton & Clayton employees in the 1880s.

BOATWOMEN'S CRAFTS

CLOTHES

Many boatwomen made their own and their families' clothes, working with hand-operated sewing machines. Other boaters' clothes were made to order by men and women in canalside villages such as Braunston, on the Grand Union Canal in Northamptonshire. The Boaters' Missions, in London, Birmingham and Worcester, also supplied clothing to boaters. Much of this was second-hand children's clothing coming from the towns where the missions were operating.

Boatwomen wore skirts that reached to their ankles, full enough to enable them to walk and to jump on and off boats comfortably, but not so full as to get in the way. In winter the skirts were of dark serge or wool, but in summer they were made of heavy cotton, sometimes striped, decorated with tucks and rows of ribbon or braid. Sometimes the stripes of the fabric were cut diagonally to form the decorative bands on the skirts.

Above the skirt, with its handspan waist, they wore coloured blouses. In the 1890s these had leg-of-mutton sleeves. Some blouses were tucked vertically at the shoulders or horizontally across the chest; other blouses were roughly smocked or shirred on the shoulders, giving a yoke effect.

Over the skirt boatwomen wore a long apron without a bib front. Some of the aprons had wide waistbands buttoned at the back and a narrow belt was worn over them. Sometimes the women wore a wide leather belt, sometimes no belt at all, for a well-fastened apron string could hold a windlass as firmly as a belt.

The pride of the boatwoman's costume was her bonnet. Made originally like a Midlands farmworker's sun-bonnet, it was lined and worn like a hat, summer and winter, with the brim tipped well forwards over the eyes, the crown on the top of the

19

A boater's family on the 'Urmston' during 1922. The older woman is wearing a black apron and black bonnet, both signs of mourning at the death of Queen Victoria. The black bonnets outlasted the mourning period because the older, more conservative boatwomen wore them into the 1920s. Younger women, many of whom returned to white bonnets in 1902, had often discarded their bonnets by 1919 in favour of fashionable hats or berets.

head and the strings tied behind the head, never under the chin. A carefully placed hat pin could help hold the bonnet in place.

In the 1880s and 1890s bonnets were made of plain white cotton or coloured, flower-sprigged cotton, either light or dark. Sprigged bonnets were trimmed with crocheted lace or plain coloured bindings. In 1901, when Queen Victoria died, many boatwomen made themselves black bonnets as a sign of mourning. They continued to wear these into the 1920s, when they were described as the boatwoman's 'traditional' bonnet. Some boatwomen returned to wearing white bonnets trimmed with broderie anglaise edgings in the years before the First World War, but the sprigged ones never regained their popularity.

This lace-trimmed, flower-printed bonnet was made by Karen Lea in the mid 1980s as a copy of those described to her as being worn by the mother and grandmother of Mrs May Russon and her elder sister Nellie. Both these women were born and brought up on boats in the first half of the twentieth century. They greatly helped and advised Karen Lea in making replicas of traditional boaters' clothes. Her first replica bonnets were too plain and the elderly sisters advised her to 'put more lace on them – boat girls were proud of their bonnets'.

In the 1890s boatmen wore either corduroy trousers and jackets with plain velvet collars, or dark, small-checked cloth suits. With both they wore matching waistcoats which were often worn unbuttoned like boleros, especially in the summer when they discarded their jackets for work. The corduroy waistcoats were single-breasted with brass buttons right to the top, where they had small stand-up collars. The cloth waistcoats had roll collars or wide revers and were double-breasted. Other, single-breasted cloth waistcoats were made with a keyhole-shaped neck opening. Waistcoats were cut straight across at the waist, without points in front in the 1880s and 1890s. After the turn of the century waistcoats with points in front gradually became more common.

Men's shirts were collarless and made of striped cotton or a wool and cotton mixture. These shirts were tunic-cut with a front opening set into a panel. Sometimes the panel was tucked vertically parallel with the buttons.

Boatmen wore both belts and braces, the latter to keep their trousers up and the former to act as a body strap to hold their windlass. Their trousers were cut with 'front falls' and bell bottoms and often had no pockets. Their belts were either wide leather, or, for best wear, linen embroidered in a pattern of colourful squares filled in with a woven 'spiderweb' of silk or wool threads. The heavy fabric was doubled over at the back to form a continuous pocket circling the waist. These belts were most popular about 1900 and after.

Instead of a collar boatmen wore a neckerchief, folded round the neck over the shirt band. Some neckerchiefs were very large and were worn crossed in front, with the two ends pulled out through the arm-

Boat families waiting by their horses at Berkhamsted in 1905. One woman wears a black bonnet, the other, by the darker horse, a white one. The two girls on the lock beam wear white bonnets and aprons; the smaller of the two has her bonnet strings undone and hanging over her bodice. The youngest girl wears the sleeveless overall worn by most girls in the 1890s and early 1900s. She also has a woollen cap on her head. The boy wears a small round cap and a loose-fitting, long-sleeved, knitted pullover.

This figure of a young boatman is part of the costume display in the Canal Museum at Stoke Bruerne. Dressed in a dark cloth suit and a waistcoat with a 'keyhole' neckline, he represents a number one of the 1890s. The figure is short, for few of the nineteenth-century boaters were tall. His 'Kingsman' neckerchief is folded and crossed at the front of his neck although the ends, pulled out through the armholes of his waistcoat, cannot be seen under his jacket. In summer the boatmen discarded their jackets and carried their windlasses hooked in the back of their belts, leaving their waistcoats unbuttoned in order to reach the windlass easily. In colder weather the windlass was worn over the shoulder, tucked into the back of the jacket.

headscarves were worn in bad weather. After 1914 most children went bareheaded.

EMBROIDERY

Many of the women and girls living on the boats in the 1890s were good at embroidery, decorating their own and their families' clothes. The stitches used were those known to all working women of the time, namely feather stitch, chainstitch and spiderwebs. The boatwomen embroidered the edges of the front panel on the men's shirts with scarlet or blue feather stitching and this bright colouring showed in glimpses below the unbuttoned waistcoat.

Some worked lines of chainstitch and feather stitching on their own blouses.

However, the embroidery most associated with the canals is that on the colourful 'spiderweb' belts worn for best by the boatmen. These consisted of three or four rows of spiderweb wheels separated by lines of chainstitch or feather stitching. These wide belts had two buckles on one end and two straps on the other, worn with the straps at one side of the waist. The origin of these belts is unknown, but many were made by boat girls for their fathers in the years between 1900 and 1913.

holes of the waistcoat. This type was known as the Kingsman. Small neckerchiefs were tied in front, with the ends left hanging. Boots and a flat cap completed the outfit for the number ones. Large caps were stiffened inside with a wire round the widest part. Company men, who were sometimes supplied with uniforms, often wore bowler hats. Caps and hats were worn both summer and winter.

Children, especially boys, wore scaleddown versions of adults' clothes. Often these were literally 'cut down' from their fathers' clothes. During the 1890s working-class girls wore back-fastening loose overalls over their dresses and boat girls followed suit. Aprons or overalls kept the clothes beneath them clean and were easier to wash.

Small babies were usually very well dressed, clothes being saved and reused from one child to the next. Bonnets were worn by girls in the 1890s, but not after the first few years of the twentieth century. School caps, hats, berets and even

The hands of Karen Lea, working at 'spiderweb' embroidery on a boatman's belt. Each 'web' is made by backstitching in a circle over a grid of eight spokes within a square. Extra stitches at each corner square the circle. Many of these belts were embroidered on to checked tea-towels, for the grids for the squares were already woven into the cloth. As the finished product, in chain-stitched belts, was solid surface embroidery, the fabric does not show when the belt is finished and made up. With feather-stitched belts, the circles were not squared and the background fabric, usually an unbleached calico or linen, can be seen. There are almost as many variations in examples of original boatmen's belts as there are belts. As with the replica bonnets (see page 20, bottom) Karen Lea was given help and advice on making boatmen's belts by Nellie Edwards and May Russon. Nellie made many belts herself as a young boat girl and remembered receiving 'ten bob a time for them belts'.

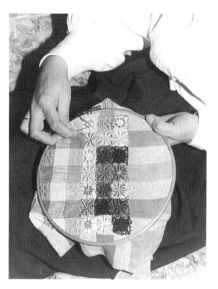

A boatman wearing a spiderweb belt, c.1910. He appears to be wearing it over a double-breasted waistcoat, although it may be that the waistcoat, which is cut straight across the bottom, is very short so that the belt shows below it. In this belt the background fabric is left showing. This photograph is from a collection of canal photographs made by Colonel Ritchie, which is now part of the British Waterways archives.

Right: A chainstitch and spiderweb-stitch belt made by the author in 1987; below it is a pair of six-stranded plaited wool braces made by Mrs Kath Irving in the mid 1980s (see page 6, top). Many of the number ones wore these brightly coloured wool braces as well as the embroidered belts. Others wore braces made of linen webbing which were occasionally embroidered with spiderwebs. The leather straps for the belts and the leather ends for the braces could be bought at any working-class haberdasher's shop. 'String' belts are sometimes mentioned by elderly boatmen when reminiscing. These could have been knotted macramé work – literally made of string – or of crochet work and would have been fastened by leather straps as used on the embroidered belts. They seem to predate the latter and none has survived.

CROCHETWORK

The most popular craft among the boatwomen was crochetwork. Crochet was first introduced into England in the 1850s, but by the 1880s it was popular with all social classes, especially the working classes. Called 'poor man's lace', it enabled individuals to produce a lace-like edging or fabric very quickly. In the 1880s it was used to make 'lace' edging to be stitched to bonnets and aprons. When

boat also had its strip of crochet as an edging. The boatwomen passed the patterns on to each other by demonstration and comparison. The cabin lace was worked in filet crochet, using a series of square holes and blocks to form a strip with a short repeating pattern. This often had pointed vandyked edging on one side and a straight edge on the other.

Crochet was also used after 1900 to make woollen shawls, plain white for

Examples of cabin lace, copied from the designs of cabin lace in the Boat Museum, Ellesmere Port, by Janet Reeve. (Top, left) The lace in the boat 'Gifford'. (Centre and bottom left) Lace in the museum store. (Right) This pattern was drafted by studying the photographs of the inside of Fred and Rose Gibbs's cabin published in 'Narrowboat Painting' by A. J. Lewery.

cheap machine-made lace became available in the 1890s, this was purchased for the bonnets and crochet was used to decorate the interior of the boat cabin, edging the curtains shielding the 'bed-hole', and acting as a trim to the shelf above the range. Every other smaller shelf in the

babies, but brightly coloured shoulder shawls for the adult women. These were crocheted in alternating stripes of light and dark colours round a small central square. The finished shawls were a yard (90 cm) square and were folded diagonally for wear.

Butty boats had no windows in their cabins, but motor boats had circular 'porthole' windows in their engine-rooms. Boatwomen crocheted circular covers for these portholes and they were held in place by hoops of wire against the inside of the glass. Some porthole covers were simple lace circles, crocheted outward from the centre, but others were crocheted pictures on the castle theme or portraits of dogs. Like the cabin lace, they were made in filet crochet to a very high standard. This replica example, featuring a church tower and cottages, was photographed at the Wendover Arm Canal Festival in May 1993.

A boathorse in traditional harness, feeding from a painted nose can. The large wooden beads covering the ropes along the flanks of the horse show up well. They were usually brightly coloured in red, yellow and green. Most canal horses were fed from metal cans. As the horses were fed while pulling the boat, the can acting as a muzzle to stop the horse grazing as it went along, these cans received rougher treatment than other painted ware. Surviving examples are often battered and dented. This horse is also wearing horse brasses and a crocheted earcap.

THE BOATHORSE

The boathorse provided the power for all boats until the 1880s, when experiments were made with steamboats. This was not very successful, because a steam engine took up too much cargo space. The semi-Bolinder diesel engine, introduced in 1906, was much more suitable for canal boats and gradually replaced horses over a period of forty years.

Some number one boatmen used a pair

The horse's earcaps were crocheted in four pieces: two cones for the ears, the face piece and the back piece. Both the last two were crocheted from side to side. The ear pieces were crocheted in the round, starting at the point and increasing the number of stitches round by round until they were long enough and wide enough to fit the horse. The four pieces were then sewn together along the top and trimmed with as many different coloured tassels as could be added, including two each side on short cords. (Top) An early twentieth-century earcap from the Canal Museum at Stoke Bruerne. (Bottom) A modern replica made by Mrs Marjorie Turpin for the Boat Museum, Ellesmere Port.

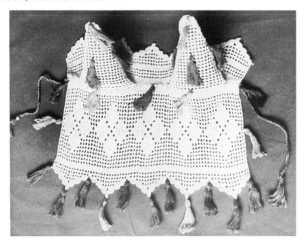

of donkeys or mules in place of a horse, but horses were more popular and were treated well by the families of the number ones, for the horse was their most valuable possession after the boat.

HARNESS

Boathorse harness differed from that of carthorses. There were no shafts and the tow-rope of the boat was attached to a hook on a curved bar called a swingletree, which hung behind the horse's hind legs. Straps across the back supported the traces connecting this to the collar. These traces were threaded through large, brightly coloured wooden bobbins, or through a leather sleeve, to protect the flanks of the horse from chafing by the rope.

HORSES' EARCAPS

In summer, when horses might be tormented by flies and other insects, the boatwomen crocheted white earcaps, decorated with coloured tassels, to put on the horses' heads. As the horse flicked its ears, the dancing tassels helped to keep away the insects.

A carte-de-visite of a boat girl, taken at Brentford c.1908, shows her wearing a leg-of-mutton sleeved blouse that had been high fashion for working women about 1896. She wears gold hoop earrings, a pearl necklace and a brooch, which may be three pearls or three gold domes mounted side by side on a bar. The plaited cord over her chest is part of a smacking whip (its handle shows over her right shoulder) which was cracked in fog, at bridges or bends in the canal, to warn others that the boat was coming. Her bonnet is white and highly frilled.

BOATERS' COLLECTABLES

PERSONAL ADORNMENT

Like all Victorians, the boatmen were collectors, accumulating items with no function other than decoration. Living in such a small space as the boat cabin restricted them to things that could be displayed in the cabin, on the horse or on their own persons. Every boatwoman had a brooch, used to fasten the collar of her blouse or hold her shawl in place. Most of them wore earrings in pierced ears. Quite often these were of real gold, given to them as wedding presents by proud young husbands. This liking for personal ornaments may well be why the boatman's embroidered belt was so popular.

HORSE AND OTHER BRASSES

The boaters called their brass items 'bright bits' and those who had them kept them shining. Horse brasses have a long history; they originated as pagan amulets to protect the animals from evil. Early nineteenth-century horse brasses were simple crosses, rosettes or wheels and these remained popular with boatmen. A cutwork wheel or crescent-shaped 'facepiece' hung on the horse's forehead, and other brasses hung on the martingale down the chest of the horse. Late-nineteenth century horse brasses had more complex designs representing heraldic devices. Others commemorated royal jubilees, the coronation of Edward VII or military victories of the Boer War. Up to the First World War horse brasses were made of solid brass. Modern brasses, sold in canal gift shops, are souvenirs of holiday trips,

A boathorse dressed up for a horse show. Boaters took part in horse shows on May Day, at Whitsun and during the wakes weeks in the Potteries towns. This horse is wearing a martingale decorated with small bells, each hanging in a bell-shaped frame. It also has a crescent-shaped brass on its forehead and highly polished buckles and harness rings. Other boathorses wore 'wheel' brasses and concentric bosses on circular bases (see page 25).

Two modern brasses, purchased at a canalside gift shop, featuring the crests and names of the Monmouthshire & Brecon Canal in Wales and Autherley Junction on the Shropshire Union and Staffordshire & Worcestershire canals.

usually bearing the arms, or at least the name, of particular canals, junctions or wharves. These designs were not necessarily used as real horse brasses.

Horse harness often had small brass studs at intervals on many of the straps. These, the harness buckles and the strips of brass round the cabin chimney were polished regularly by the boaters. Many

boatwomen also had 'bright bits' in the cabins, miniature windlasses being very popular. The base of the oil lamp used for lighting in the cabin was of brass, as was the drying rail above the range.

LACE PLATES

Lace plates have a series of holes pierced round the rim through which a

28

A lace plate of the 1870s or 1880s showing a transfer drawing of Great Yarmouth. The plate is pink and white with touches of gold round the fretting. This plate is in the Boat Museum at Ellesmere Port.

A lace plate of about 1907 with a painting of fruit in the centre. It is a typical Edwardian plate.

A modern lace plate made by John Branch, a potter who lives on the narrowboat 'Hale Lady', to celebrate the bicentenary of the Grand Junction Canal – later renamed the Grand Union. It shows the seal of the Grand Junction Canal Committee of 1793.

29

ribbon may be threaded to hang them up. Some were made in the potteries of the Midlands, but many others were imported from Bohemia. They were always intended for display and many Victorian households would have had at least one such plate hung on a wall. Most narrowboat families had several, arranged in vertical rows by the side of the range and table/cupboard, or hung against the pelmet over the 'bed-hole'. The pictures on these plates included fruit, flowers, views of well-known towns and portraits.

MEASHAM TEAPOTS

These large teapots, with smaller teapots forming the knob on the lid, were so popular with the boaters that they have come to be known as 'barge teapots', in spite of the fact that boaters hated being called 'bargees'. The pots were brown-glazed and ornamented with moulded fruit, flowers and birds. Bands of lettering (black on white) carried mottoes or the name of the owner. These teapots were made to order and a boatman could specify the motto and the name, then pay off the cost, a little at a time, each journey past the agent. The teapot would not necessarily be used every day, but would be brought out for special occasions and family celebrations.

Other items displayed in boat cabins might include glazed pottery pairs of 'cottage dogs' or pottery figures. All these, and decorated tableware, were made in Staffordshire and were popular with working folk and cottage dwellers all round England. They played an obvious part in the boaters' lives because of the compact size of the boat cabins, the boatwomen, being proud of their one-roomed homes, putting all their ornaments on display at once.

A Measham teapot in the Canal Museum at Stoke Bruerne. Wares of this kind, originally known as Rockingham teapots, were first made about 1870 at Pool Village in south Derbyshire. By 1890 they were being sold in a grocery shop at Cut End, Measham, Leicestershire, where they became popular with the boaters. Later they could be ordered at several places along the canal, but the boaters always called them Measham teapots after the place they first saw them. The potters, Mason and Cash, continued to produce these teapots until 1939.

30

CONCLUSION

Although the preceding descriptions may give the impression that the boaters lived so that they could be seen whatever they were doing, it must be remembered that they were as concerned for their privacy as everyone else. It was considered very bad manners to look into the cabin of a boat or to step across the deck without asking permission. To be invited into a boat cabin was a great honour. The narrowboats were people's homes as well as their means of livelihood. 'An Englishman's home is his castle' was as true of the boaters as of any other families. They painted castles on their boats and their possessions, but they did it for their own pride and pleasure, not for public acclaim. If it made them distinctive they were proud of it, but they did not care if others disliked it. The painted boats and artefacts were a true folk art, born out of the lives of those who produced it, something particularly English. Today it is enjoying a revival, a hundred years after its heyday.

The arts of the canals are still alive and workers in all the aspects discussed in this book may be found at any canal festival. This artist, painting a small water barrel, was photographed at the Wendover Arm Festival in May 1993.

Derek Pearson demonstrating rope-fender making at the Wendover Arm Festival, May 1993.

31

FURTHER READING

Burton, Anthony. *The Great Days of the Canals*. David & Charles, 1989.
Hill, John M. *Narrowboat Decoration*. Birmingham Canal Navigation Society, 1983.
Lewery, A.J. *Narrow Boat Painting*. David & Charles, 1986.
Lewery, Tony. *Flowers Afloat*. David & Charles, 1996.
Reeves, Janet M. *Cabin Lace*. (Available at canal museums and from the Inland Waterways Association), 1989.
Smith, Donald. *Boats and Boaters*. Hugh Evelyn, 1973.
Smith, Donald. *Horse on the Cut*. Patrick Stephens, 1982.
Stewart, Sheila. *Ramlin Rose*. Oxford University Press, 1993.
Vince, John. *Discovering Horse Brasses*. Shire Publications, reprinted 1994.
Young, Anne. *Paint Roses and Castles*. David & Charles, 1993.

LEAFLETS
Pattern for Boatman's Belt. Available from the Canal Museum, Stoke Bruerne; the Boat Museum, Ellesmere Port; and the National Waterways Museum, Gloucester; or direct from the author, c/o Shire Publications, Cromwell House, Church Street, Princes Risborough, Buckinghamshire HP27 9AA.
Patterns for English Sunbonnets (including a boatwoman's bonnet). Available from Elmbridge Museum, Church Street, Weybridge, Surrey KT13 8DE.
Patterns for Horses' Ear-Caps. Available from the Canal Museum, Stoke Bruerne.

PLACES TO VISIT

Intending visitors are advised to find out the times of opening and to check that relevant items are on show before travelling.

Black Country Museum, Tipton Road, Dudley, West Midlands DY1 4SQ. Telephone: 0121-557 9643.
Boat Museum, South Pier Road, Ellesmere Port, Cheshire L65 4FW. Telephone: 0151-355 5017.
Canal Museum, Canal Street, Nottingham NG1 7ET. Telephone: 0115-959 8835.
Canal Museum, Stoke Bruerne, Towcester, Northamptonshire NN12 7SE. Telephone: 01604 862229.
London Canal Museum, 12/13 New Wharf Road, Kings Cross, London N1 9RT. Telephone: 0171-713 0836.
National Waterways Museum, Llanthony Warehouse, The Docks, Gloucester GL1 2EH. Telephone: 01452 318054.

Many smaller, local canal museums and heritage centres can be found along the waterways system. Typical examples are at Devizes, Wiltshire; Llangollen, Clwyd; Shardlow, Derbyshire; and Welshpool, Powys. There are many others.

Canal gift shops at basins, junctions and popular locks sell modern versions of traditional canal arts. Such shops may be found on the Birmingham waterways, in Coventry Basin, at Braunston, Northamptonshire, and at the bottom of Foxton locks near Market Harborough, Leicestershire. There are very many others.